PHONES, ELECTRONIC DEVICES, AND YOU:

Who Is in Charge?

Eric Tangumonkem, Ph.D.

IEM PRESS

Richardson, Texas

ISBN 10: 1-63603-017-3
ISBN 13: 978-1-63603-017-3

Library of Congress Catalog Card Number: 2019953639

Table of Contents

Dedication

To my wife and children for their encouragement, support, and proper use of electronic devices.

To all who are struggling to bring their electronic devices under control. You have what it takes to be in charge, not your devices.

Introduction

The last thing I do each night is to turn off my phone and put it away. Most of the time, it is left in the living room. This was not my practice, but after reading and hearing about the negative effects of spending too much time on the screen and the negative impact of the phone on relationships, plus the fact that I am not a 911 dispatcher or a fire station chief, there was no point sleeping with my phone on. More importantly, I do not want the phone to interfere in my matrimonial bed.

It is true that this device has become part and parcel of our lives, and it is connecting us in ways unimaginable. Unfortunately, it is causing a lot of havoc in our relationships because one cannot have meaningful connections with somebody and be on the phone at the same time. While many studies have focused on the issue of phone addiction and the influence of the phone on the brain, this book is going to focus solely on the influence of the phone on the quality of our relationships and interactions with other people.

Nobody is going to control and police your phone use because it is a touchy issue. Therefore, you have to be proactive and take action. Most of us have made the phone more important than it really is. Some even have separation anxiety without them. It has gotten so bad that you hear people talking of phone fasting. *This issue seems to be driven by some unwritten law, which demands that we must remain connected at all times.*

The question is, must we be connected to the Internet at all times? The phone used to be a tool to call people and talk with them, but it has morphed into an all-in-one watch, computer, calculator, camera, camcorder, speedometer, compass, GPS navigation system, a library, record player, online shopper, etc. There is so much that we can do with the phone these days that was unimaginable a few years ago. Right now, you do not even need to press anything; you can just talk to it, and the phone will do whatever you want.

This is to underscore the fact that the phone is an essential tool and occupies an important place in our lives. That said, we must place the phone in its proper place, or it will become a curse instead of a blessing. It can become a serious impediment to our relationships and interactions with other people. You do not want this because one of the most important activities we do is connecting with other humans and having healthy relationships.

Here is an opportunity to learn how to use the phone properly and placing it in its proper place. Instead of the phone becoming a hindrance, it will enhance your relationships and improve them. You will be expected to make some changes because if you keep doing what you are doing right now, you will get the same results. I hope that you will cherish your relationships above all else and reap the benefits of doing what is right for you, your family, your friends and connections.

Chapter 1:
The Comment

I had arrived on time for my Geology class and all my students were already waiting for me to open the lab so they can get in. When I arrived, the key that I had did not work. I started searching frantically in my bag. After what appears to be a long time but actually less than a couple of minutes, I gave up in frustration.

I decided to call the campus police to come and open the door for us to get into the lab. While we were waiting, most of the students were on their phones doing one thing or another.

After what seemed like forever, the police officer arrived.

As he proceeded to open the door, he asked, "Who is the professor?" I answered, "I am the one."

Then he asked, "Is that why you are the only one who is not on the phone?"

It was a rhetorical question, and he was not expecting an answer. This police officer was making a powerful comment that was summarizing a scene that has become ubiquitous everywhere you go.

It is not uncommon to find people either sitting or walking with their eyes fixated on the phone they are holding. This obsession with electronic gadgets is becoming a problem, and many are already having a lot of issues with phone addiction.

The other day, I saw a woman fall into a huge dumpster that was on the street because she was checking her phone and not paying attention to where she was going. It was so bad that she broke some bones. There are many of these horror stories all over the Internet, and a day does not pass by without hearing something that makes your skin crawl.

Thousands have died because they are texting while driving, and this has forced some states to pass laws banning phone use while operating a motor vehicle. In spite of these laws, people are still texting while driving and some are still talking on their phones while driving. There were parents and teenagers who didn't come home to their families because their lives were cut short.

When you consider the cost of all the dreams that have been killed by the reckless use of phones and other electronic gadgets, it will make you think twice before texting the next time you are behind the wheel. In addition to deaths, injuries, and missed opportunities, you have to factor in the marriages and relationships that have been ruined.

This book was written not to bash phones and electronic devices but to help you put them in the right place when it comes to your interactions with other people.

It does not matter how many thousands of friends you have on LinkedIn, Twitter, Facebook, Snapchat, Instagram, etc. The friends that truly count are those who will pick up the phone when you call them. These will be those you meet face to face and have coffee or tea with. Even if you have not met them in person but have exchanged phone numbers and speak to each other constantly, these are the individuals that truly count, and you have to treat these relationships with care.

Many people are operating on the misguided notion of multitasking. Many studies have debunked multitasking, yet people still try to do it. You may be talking on the phone, watching TV, and checking your email all at the same time, but our brains are not wired to do that. You may pride yourself on multitasking, but all you are doing is reducing your efficiency and productivity.

The students that struggle in my classes are those who are always juggling between their phones and electronic devices while trying to follow my lectures. According to these students, they are present in class, but the truth of the matter is that they are physically present in the room, but their minds are elsewhere. They are trying to have it both ways, but that is not possible. You always end up sacrificing something if you try to do too many different things at the same time.

When I was a kid, my parents drove this lesson deep in my psyche: they had never heard about multitasking but understood that you could not chase two rabbits and catch them at the same time. If you try that, you will lose both rabbits.

This brings to mind an ethnic group in the Kalahari that chases down game to exhaustion, then kill it for food. They do not try to chase the entire herd of antelope but will separate the male from the rest of the group because it has long and heavy horns and will tire easily. After separating the male antelope from the rest of the herd, these men will start the chase that may last up to eight hours. The men literally chase the male antelope until it becomes too tired to run and just collapses from exhaustion. The men will then spear the animal.

The men succeed in doing something like this because of focus. If they try to chase the entire herd, they will be running in too many different directions, and it will make them unsuccessful, to say the least. They will fail not because they do not have the energy or stamina to run, but because they are not focused and are spread thin.

What has chasing rabbits got to do with phone use and your quality of life? There is a lot of similarity between chasing rabbits and antelope and how you use electronic devices. The principle of focus works under all circumstances. To be effective and efficient, it is imperative that you learn to focus. Unfortunately, the phone and other electronic devices are making it almost impossible for us to focus these days.

I see this firsthand in my classes. Some of the students have their phones hidden under the desk and are browsing while the lecture is going on. I know this because occasionally, I will leave the lectern and walk around the room while delivering the lecture. The intent is to engage the students and keep them interested in the subject.

Needless to say, when a quiz is given, most of the students who are always on their phones do not do well.

In this book, I want to address an issue that many think about but do not bring up because they do not want to hurt the feelings of others. Many people ignore it and pretend the problem does not exist. But playing ostrich and hiding our heads in the sand has never solved any problem. It is high time stopped playing games. Just because you ignore something and wish it away does not mean it is going to go away. Phones and electronic devices have become an integral part of our lives, and this makes it more urgent for us to ensure that they are put in their proper place. *You* are supposed to be running the show, not your phone. If you think this is an overstatement, read on. By the end of the book, we will revisit this issue.

It is time to dig in and embark on this exciting and rewarding journey.

Chapter 2:
The Elephant in the Room

"How can we be free when we are prisoners to social media in a world without privacy? How can we be free when our every movement is tracked, and every conversation is recorded and can easily be held against us? How exactly are we free if we are tethered to our cell phones?" —Tom Green

There is an elephant in the room, and nobody wants to talk about it because it will make everybody uncomfortable. Nobody wants to appear to be meddling in other people's affairs or be too sensitive to what others are doing. Being the oddball is the last thing anybody wants. It is unfortunate that at times, we blindly follow trends for the sake of fitting in. If you dare question or raise an objection, you are shunned, labeled and called names. This should not be so because the crowd is not always right. Just because something is popular, or everybody is engaged in it, does not legitimize it.

The elephant in the room is the phone and other electronic devices. These have imposed themselves between us, our loved ones and other relationships. They give the impression that we are connected, but it is a false connection because even though we get together, we do not engage one another.

It is not uncommon to walk into a restaurant and see a family around the table all engaged with their own phones. While waiting for their food to be served, they are not talking to each other; instead, their eyes are transfixed on their phones. The father may be on LinkedIn catching up with his colleagues, the mum is on Instagram checking pictures and at the same time checking out Pinterest for something to buy. Their two children are jumping from Facebook to Snapchat, YouTube, etc.

The phone and electronic devices have become ubiquitous. They have taken a life of their own and are issuing the orders for us to follow. We are supposed to master them, but they are mastering us. No wonder families get together, but all they do is focus on their phones and electronic devices. Some even text each other even though they are in the same room.

Are you surprised by the level of unhealthy exchanges that are taking place on Facebook and other social media platforms? You just need to read the comment section of any online newspaper, blog post, or YouTube video to experience firsthand the lack of civility that has become so prevalent in our day. Many people think that they can hide behind their computer screens or phones and post whatever comes to their minds. Nothing reveals people's true character and intent than some of these posts. Because nobody sees these individuals, they say whatever they want. This is an unfortunate development and points out one of the great flaws of the information superhighway. These days, gossip spreads at the speed of light, character assassination has become mainstream, and fake news is the norm.

There is no telling the havoc and destruction our modern communication devices and how we interact with them is causing. Some husbands are closer to their phones than their wives. They cling to the phone all day, and when they get home, they still cannot let go of it. You can see them texting, answering calls, and moving from one social media platform to the other. They think they are being cool and connected. Some insist that they need to keep up with what is happening.

The question is at what expense? Are you willing to sacrifice your marriage and children on the altar of keeping up with the times? How can you justify neglecting your wife and your children because you are chatting with and texting people who will not be there when you need them the most?

I can hear the protest that I must have been hired by your wife to get into your business. Your wife did not hire me. If your wife is already complaining, you MUST listen to her. Cut back on how much time you are investing in social media, texting and talking on your phone. It seems that you have forgotten that you only have 24 hours and how you spend your time reveals what is truly important to you. How can you keep saying that your wife and children are important to you when you continue to neglect them and spend your time on something else? This issue of neglecting marriages, children and relationships are not restricted to the husbands. The wives are also committing the same offense. You spend so many hours looking at pictures of your lady friends and their children on Facebook, Instagram and other social media platforms to the extent that your husbands come home from work and you have no time to welcome them back.

When you get on the phone with your friends, the conversations go on and on as if you have all the time in the world. The saddest thing is that this time is spent talking about others, which adds little or no value to your life. You just wasted another one hour that you could have invested in reading a good book that will improve your marriage or watched a talk that will help you raise successful children.

What in the world are you thinking when you spend so much time browsing through other people's pictures instead of building yourself up? What are you looking for, and when will you realize that this habit is not helping you? You only have 24 hours, and there is so much that you need to be doing. Allowing the phone and social media to distract you will hamper you from becoming all you were created to be. Now is the time to prioritize spending quality time with your family and loved ones. You say you love them, yet you spend little time with them.

Children are guilty of this bad habit as well. They are on these devices all the time. Their parents must call them multiple times to come to attend to some important duty because they are distracted. When they are on their electronic devices, nothing else matters, and they do not care.

How can you justify going to class and spending most of the time on your phone or iPad and not paying attention to what the lecturer is saying? Some of you are being sponsored by your parents, and you are wasting these valuable family resources by not maximizing your time in class.

You may be saying that it is your life, and whatever you do is your business and has nothing to do with anybody. If this is what you think, I am sorry to tell you that you are seriously mistaken in being so selfish. Nobody is an island; we are all interdependent on each other, even those who are not related to us. It is crucial that we factor in the success of others in our own success equation. You have to succeed because the success of others depends on your success. If you fail, you are not only failing yourself, you are failing all the other people that are depending on you succeeding.

For example, the plan may be for you to get into medical school and you allow your phone and electronic devices to prevent you from getting the score that is necessary for you to enter medical school. This implies that all the patients you were supposed to help in the future will never be helped because you failed to go to medical school.

You may be saying, "But other people made it into medical school and took care of the patients I was supposed to care for." The question I have for you is, "Are you somebody else?" You are unique and different. You should never exchange yourself for anybody else. It is impossible for you to be somebody else.

If the fear of failing and the great impact on others are not enough to push you to succeed, maybe the following will make you think about how important our connectivity and dependence on each other is. Imagine for a minute that your current dentist failed to get into dentistry school, and your family doctor did not make it as well, who will take care of your health? You may argue that other dentists and doctors will. What if these other doctors and dentists failed?

What if all the mechanics failed, the lawyers, accountants, machinists, carpenters, builders, truck drivers, chemists, biologists, geologists, physicists, professors, etc. failed? Let us take it even further and assume that you were the only person on earth. How will you function? Who will build your house, repair your car, provide you with fuel, and treat you when you get sick? You are getting the picture, right?

We need each other, and it is important that each one of us succeeds in our specialty because the success of others depends on us and our success depends on their success. In short, we need each other, and it is a selfish thing to say that, "It is my life and I can do whatever I want with it, including wasting time on my phone and social media." Let me remind you that it is not just your life. Next time you are tempted to get distracted by your phone, remember all the other people who are depending on you to succeed and will fail if you failed, all because you allowed the phone and your electronic devices to control you instead of you controlling them.

We all appear to be "working" all the time, and this can be seen by how much time we spend on our phones. Are we really more productive or we are distracted? I am not going to answer this question for you, but I suggest that you ensure that when you are on the phone, you are actually doing things that are in line with the goals that you have set for your life.

It is a waste of time to spend valuable time on social media, checking out pictures and making derogatory comments on blog posts and newspaper articles just because you can. It is important to hold yourself accountable. Before you write anything and click the Send or Post button, you have to be sure that you can read what you have written in front of your children, family, and friends. If in doubt, do not send or post it. Any discomfort is a sign that what you have written is not edifying.

Now that we have put the spotlight on the elephant in the room, we can talk about it and see how to deal with it before it tramples all of us. The phone and other electronic devices can be vicious and uncompromising taskmasters, demanding that you are engaged with them all the time. There have been cases of people who have binge-played video games without rest or breaks for hours on end, and when their bodies could no longer take it, they collapsed and died of exhaustion.

While the illustration given above may seem extreme, it is shocking how many marriages are being torn apart because of one or both parties are always on their phones.

For lack of a better word, they have become addicted to their phones. Like any addict, all they care about is the "high" they get from their drug of choice. While they are on their phone, everything else can wait, and they couldn't care less about what might happen. This is an unfortunate situation that must be addressed.

The rest of this book will continue exposing this modern slave master and tyrant, and I will present ways of breaking free and learning to control our phones and electronic devices instead of them controlling you. It is imperative that you get back in control. If you don't, you are in for a lot of surprises.

Chapter 3:
The Guest

"The dirty little secret that nobody likes to talk about is that things just might have been better before the Internet. We had more time to ourselves before cell phones and text messaging and Facebook consumed our lives." —Tom Green

Your friends come over to visit you. They were talking on their phones. They stop for a second, long enough to exchange words of welcome. Then, they go back to the phone and keep talking to whoever they were talking with. You wait and wait for them to come off the phone to no avail. As soon as they get off the phone, they start texting while trying to hold a conversation with you. You can tell immediately that they are distracted but being a polite host, you do not want to hurt their feelings and make them feel uncomfortable. So, you do not tell them to get off the phone.

How can anybody blame you for being a good host and not interfering in your visitors' affairs? Who knows?

They may be handing some life-changing transaction. You are perfectly correct not to interfere or try to correct them because you are not the phone police. It is not your place to tell your guest what to do or not do with their phone.

This is where this book comes in. This is going to be your voice and the voices of all the other people who welcome guests in their homes. It is a reminder to the visitor of what is the right and polite thing to do when you go to visit somebody. It is totally impolite to walk in while on the phone, and when you get there, have the audacity to continue talking on the phone. You visit people because you want to connect with them. One way to connect is to be an active listener, and it is impossible to be texting, watching YouTube videos, and listening actively at the same time.

The rule of thumb is that when you decide to go visit somebody, you have to give them the respect and priority by focusing on them, not on your phone. You came to talk to them and fellowship together. Therefore, you should not allow the phone to come between you and your host.

If you are not an emergency responder or on call, it is a good practice to turn off your phone and put it away when you walk into the house. Not putting the phone away makes you vulnerable to the temptation of checking the phone while trying to engage your host at the same time.

Do not forget that your host has set aside valuable time to talk with you, and it is important that you respect their time by being physically and emotional present. There is no way you can be on the phone and connecting at the same time. You may feel that you are connecting because you are there in person, but the way we are wired makes it impossible. Many people are under the illusion that they have it both ways. This is a myth and it does not work!

The case of Roland

Roland is always on his phone, even when he goes to visit his friends. His justification is that he needs to get work done. He will drive to his friend's house, come back, and not remember what took him there in the first place because the whole time he was there, he was texting, browsing the Internet, and answering calls. Even when they are at the table eating, it is not uncommon for him to be talking on the phone as well. His attitude has been troubling his close friend for some time, but the friend does not know how to bring this to his attention. The few times that the subject has come up, Roland has been quick to point out all the pressing things that he has to do over the phone.

As time went on, Roland's persistent use of the phone started tearing the fabric of his friendships. Even though they get together, there is no connection. No wonder Roland got up one day and realized that he was a loner because his friends had slowly drifted away. People like to connect with others, that is why they get together. It is sad that some sit down and text each other, instead of talking directly to one another.

Roland's bad habit destroyed his friendships, yet he was unrepentant and did not see the need to change. His phone was his best buddy, but when he came upon hard times, Roland could not turn to his phone for comfort. He needed people to talk with. Fortunately for him, his friends came to his aid and gave him the support and encouragement that he needed.

Before you go to visit a friend, make sure that you have cleared your plate and ready to connect with them.

If you are not on call, turn off your phone and put it away. You may have to leave the phone in your car if you drove there. If not, turn off your phone and do not turn it on until you leave. This may sound drastic, but it will improve the quality of your life and relationships that you are having.

Bad habits die hard, and you should not deceive yourself that you will have your phone on and not look at it or use it. The best and prudent thing to do is to turn it off and put it away. Do not mute or put it on silent mode. Turn off the phone!

"But why should I turn off my phone if other people are having theirs on and are using it?" Excellent question. While it may appear unfair that other people may be using their phones, not using your phone will send a strong message to all those present and will eventually bring about the change this book is all about. What is the point of friends getting together and not talking to each other?

Nothing steals time and downgrades the quality of any interaction than divided attention. It is not possible to be on the phone and be an active listener at the same time. Save yourself the embarrassment of trying to do this by turning off your phone. Be the change by setting the example. It is OK to be the only person whose phone is turned off. Sooner or later, others will ask you why and it will be an appropriate opportunity to educate them on the benefits of putting the phone in its rightful place. Instead of complaining and waiting for others to change first, you should lead the change.

In addition to being part of the solution, when you turn off your phone and other electronic devices, you earn the right to talk about the drawbacks of allowing the phone to interfere in conversation. If you want to successfully lead people somewhere, it is easier when you have been there before. It is even more powerful when you have not only been there but are willing to take others and go there with them. Action is more contagious than mere talk. People are more likely to do what they see than what they only hear about. Your action will help other people break this terrible habit of spending all their time on the phone and electronic devices while visiting.

Just because nobody is talking about the drawbacks of being on the phone when people get together to visit each other does not mean it is OK to do so. We hope that this resource will spark the conversation and help many people break free from this bad habit.

Permit me to beat a dead horse to death. You may be saying that this phone thing is not a big deal, but why is it that if you were invited to see the CEO of some company or anybody that you consider important, you will turn off your phone and pay close attention? The simple answer is that this situation demands respect. What makes you think that your friends do not need to be respected as well? Treating all people with dignity is required from all of us and your friends are not excluded. We are guilty of disrespecting them by taking them for granted. This is very unfortunate and should be discouraged. Let it start with you. Each time you plan to go visit, know that your phone must take second place. The best way to do it is by putting the phone out of sight.

Here is your opportunity to become part of the solution by setting a good example. Initially, this may feel awkward and out of place, but with time, others are going to join you. This issue of friends, families — all humans — getting together yet not talking to each and connecting is extremely serious and must be tackled. The toll that phone usage takes on relationships cannot be undermined. I hope that you will set the pace in your sphere of influence by putting away your phone and engaging those that you are visiting.

"Wait a minute. What if those I am visiting do not care and are on their own phones?" This is a legitimate question that needs to be addressed. The first step is to set the example by turning your own phone off and putting it out of sight. The first time you turn off your phone, you should not say anything about it. All you need to do is to remain silent. When you visit this friend or relative a couple of times and do not use your phone, and this does not register anything in their minds, then it is time for you to take the next action. This step is going to require some courage and tough love. We are hoping that you love your relationship with whoever is involved to the point where you are willing to "place your life on the line" for it. The only way you can proceed is to bring the issue up and talk about it.

The conversation can start as follows: "Hi, Andrew. I know how difficult it is for us not to be on our phones these days. The demand on us and our time are huge and the boundary between family time and work time is getting blurred with each passing day.

"Therefore, it is difficult to tell when one is just surfing the net or responding to important job-related emails and text messages. This is something that all of us are going through. That said, we must understand that there are other things in life that are important and may even be more important than a job. Relationships must and should be prioritized by all. How you spend your time and who you spend it with speaks volumes. I am saying this because you might have noticed that when I come over to visit, my phone is off. This does not mean that there are no pressing emails to respond to or trending news items to read or exciting YouTube videos to watch, etc.

"The reason is that I cherish our relationship and time together and do not want anything to interfere with it. You may not like what I am about to say, but when we get together, I think it will do both of us a lot of good if we turn off our phones and actually talk to each other. Please do not take it personally. I, too, struggle with putting my phone away, but I do it because our relationship is more important. What do you think?"

Your host may not want to discuss the matter, but any reasonable person will, at least, listen to you. If they do and continue ignoring you when you come over to visit, you have to escalate it by letting them know that you have better things to do than coming over and not engaging in meaningful conversation and connecting with each other. It may be time for you to reconsider the proper use of your time by limiting how much time you spend with this friend or relative of yours. Time is precious and how we spend our time impacts our level of success and achievement.

Here is an opportunity for you to redeem some time and make proper use of it. If your friend cherishes and values your friendship, they will do everything to ensure that when you get together, the time is well spent. If they refuse to listen to you, then you may be hanging out with the wrong person.

This may sound drastic, but you have to remember that surrounding yourself with the right people will determine your level of success. Maybe this is the time to make some changes and drop some people. Did I say drop some people? Yes! As painful as it may sound, you are going to make some tough choices, and this may be one of them. Your time is your life ticking away, and you cannot afford to waste it. The choice is yours to make; nobody will make it for you.

Chapter 4:
The Host

"I think technology is us, not something we invented. I think we are more psychic now because we have cell phones and you can look and see who's calling you. When people start seeing technology as us, as humanity, our whole idea of what existence is, is going to shift." —*Ryan Trecartin*

Has it occurred to you that when somebody comes to visit you, it is crucial that you engage with them? Do you know it is rude and disrespectful to be on your phone or computer when your guest comes over? Would you like to be ignored when you go to visit someone?

There is no situation that demands the golden rule more than what we are talking about here: "Do unto others what you want to be done unto you". In other words, treat other people the way you want to be treated. For example, if you want people to give you full attention and not be fidgeting with their electronic devices while you are talking to them, you should do same when others are talking to you. If you do not want to go and visit a family member or friend and be ignored, do not ignore other people.

You may be saying that the golden rule is common sense and it is preposterous to bring it up. Here is the reality: it is not uncommon to walk into a home to visit and your host takes a few minutes off the phone to welcome you, but then he or she gets back on the phone to complete the call, which seems to never end. At times, they will move on from that call to another…and another…and another. When they get off the phone, they start texting. Before you know it, they are on Facebook checking the latest trending event and giggling all along. Your guest expects you to take out your own phone and join the party of getting together but not connecting.

You feel like screaming at your host, "Dude, I am here to see you and for us to talk and catch up. There are many other important things that I have given up just to be here. Why are you not valuing my time? What is it on that phone that is more important than me? How can you treat my presence so callously? Don't you think that basic courtesy demands that you pay attention to my presence?"

By the time you finish going through these things in your head, a part of you wants to leave immediately. But you are struggling to be a good guest and not want to rock the boat too hard. After all, you are the one intruding your host's private space and have to play by their values. When in Rome, do as the Romans do.

Who will blame you for being a good guest and keeping quiet about the whole situation? That is why it is incumbent upon the host to set the tone and create a welcoming and engaging atmosphere. When you are planning to host people, the idea of multitasking has to be thrown out of the window. People are busy and have many other important things to do than come to your house and watch you play on your phone. Always remember that people have far better things to do than be treated as if they are background noise.

The visit was not forced on you. Therefore, you should do the right thing by carving out time to connect with your guest. In other words, before your guest arrives, it is important you treat the visit as an important appointment and remove all distractions.

If the President of the United States of America came to visit you, will you be on your phone? You might be saying that this is a ridiculous question because anybody in their right mind will give the President their full attention if he came to visit. The reason is that the President is extremely busy and occupies the highest office in the land and in the world. Therefore, if the President sets time aside to come and visit you, you must treat the visit with respect and dignity.

Why would you treat the visit of the President differently from that of your friends and guests? Do your friends and guests deserve less respect and attention? How do you justify this disrespect and lack of dignified treatment? Will you be happy if you went to visit and your host treats you in the same way? Always remember that all of us deserve to be treated with honor, dignity, and respect, especially if they sacrificed their time and resources to visit you. There is no justification for focusing on your phone instead of your guest.

Your guest may want to be polite and courteous and not bring up the issue of your lack of focus and engagement. Just because they are not complaining does not mean that they are not unhappy about the situation. Many do not like the fact that they invested time and resources to come and connect with you, but you ignored them. You may be thinking that they would understand because everybody is on their phones these days. Just because everybody is doing it does not mean it is the right thing to do.

The message in this chapter is simple and straightforward: if somebody comes to visit you, it is imperative that you do the following out of respect and consideration:

- Turn off your phone and connect with them.
- When they are at the door and you are on the phone, you should get off the phone, welcome your guest, and connect with them.
- There is no texting and browsing on the Internet while your guest is visiting you.
- Keep the visit short if you must attend to other pressing issues, but make sure that your guest is aware of what is going on.
- If there is an emergency, everybody will understand. Most of the time, we are on our phones not because the issues cannot wait, but it is a manifestation of a bad habit that we have cultivated.
- Turn off the television and engage with your guest. If you have something on that you want all of you to watch as part of the visit, this is fine, but it should

not be on all the time while you are trying to engage and connect with your guest.

- Be there physically and emotionally. If you fail to connect well, your guest will hesitate to come back in the future.
- If your guest is distracted by their phone or electronic device, you should politely and tactfully bring it to their attention.

It may be that you have done all to connect with your guest, but the guest is the one too distracted by their phone or electronic devices. Worse, they refuse to believe or admit that they are distracted. If this guest is somebody that you have known for a long time, it may be time for you to reduce the amount of time you are spending together. I say so because they do not value your time. If they did, they will respect that time and ensure that you connect with each other. It is not enough to be in the same room. The best way to connect is to remove all distractions and talk to each other. It is impossible to be talking to one person and responding to emails and text messages at the same time. Anybody who insists that this is their preferred way of conducting themselves should be left to do their thing, but they should not do it on your time.

The loving thing to do is to bring up this issue to the attention of all you care and love because there is so much at stake. Many people mistake avoiding inconvenience for love. They think that they love somebody if they do all not to make them feel uncomfortable. The truth is that they are being driven by self-preservation. They do not want to be rejected by their loved ones or friends and would rather let sleeping dogs lie.

Now is the time to have this crucial conversation, and you should do it without fear or remorse. If you don't, who else is going to do it? There is going to be some pushback, but you should do it anyway. Do it because you may just be saving the life of your loved one or friend. Do not allow the fact that everybody is doing it to deceive you in thinking that is it is the right thing to do. We do what is right because it is right, not because everybody is doing it.

Chapter 5:
The Family Time

"We all fall into our habits, our routines, our ruts. They're used quite often, consciously or unconsciously, to avoid living, to avoid doing the messy part of having relationships with other people, of dealing with a person next to us. That's why we can all be in a room on our cell phones and not have to deal with one another."
—*Andrew Stanton*

There is a difference between being together and connecting. Just because you are in the same room with your family does not mean that you are connecting. For connection to take place, there has to be some intentionality. Unfortunately, the phone and other electronic devices have come between many families, making the time they spend together more of alone time than connection time.

Some drastic measures have to be taken to restore healthy connection at home when the family gathers around the dinner table. Life is short, and children grow up fast. Before you know it, they have left the house. Therefore, do everything to maximize the the time that you and your children are at home. There is a lot to teach your children before they leave the house. This implies that the time you spend together has to be utilized well. Instead of everybody being on their phones and electronic devices, it is important to plan activities that the entire family can participate in. Some of these activities can involve electronic devices as we are going to see.

The rule of thumb is that, as a family, you should all have at least one meal a day during which they get to connect with each other and strengthen family bonds. In my family, we usually ask our children to share with us about their day. They all take turns talking and we, the parents, ask probing questions.

We do not answer the phone when we are at our dinner table. This is a long-established tradition, and a few of our visitors are taken aback by this. We simply tell them that we are not first responders and will attend to the call at the appropriate time. We have done this for years and have yet to miss an important appointment or information. Thank God for answering machines and voicemail that collect and store messages when we are at the dinner table. When it is time to eat, it is time to eat and connect with one another. We are setting the right example to our children that family time is an important time and should be taken seriously.

There are no electronics in the bedrooms. We have set an example by not having a television in our own room. There is a central area where all of us sit and study. This is where all the computers and laptops in the house are located. All of us sit there and do our work. I teach online and write as well.

These rules may sound archaic and outdated, but they work for us. It has made our family time productive and engaging. We take a lot of road trips, which means we spend hours upon hours on the road as we crisscross all over the United States of America. We have been to more than 25 states already and aim to visit all 50 states before all our children leave the house. During our road trips, there are times all of us are talking, then our children will take out their electronic devices and play games with each other or individually. At times, a movie is played for them to watch. The point I am making here is that we do not allow them to be on their electronic devices throughout the entire trip. There are even times when all we do is listen to music and enjoy the scenery through which we are driving.

Do not get me wrong: our children have electronic devices, but they only use them on weekends. Even the television is shut off and only turned on during the weekend. When we are at home, it is time to connect with each other and talk to one another. This is something that we do not struggle over because we instituted it when our children were young, and they have grown used to it. We are not suggesting that you break your TV set, but it is up to you to decide what quality you want your family time to be.

When you come home from work and you are not on call, turn off your phone and put it away. Make sure that you are not just there physically, but present emotionally and psychologically. It is not uncommon for parents to be at home, but not really there because they are occupied with the phones. No wonder your children are trying hard to get your attention. Instead, you are too busy interacting with people who will not even show up at your funeral. You are putting in a lot of time to chatting with people on social media, 99% of whom will not miss you when you die.

It is high time you stopped taking your family for granted and start truly connecting with them. This is a reminder that your family is more important than all the social media friends that you are trying to cater to. This is not to suggest that you should stop social media and trash your phone. On the contrary, it is important to have a strong social media presence and to put in the time and energy to build a platform, but you should not do this at the expense of your family and the relationships that truly matter in your life.

Phones and electronic devices have an important place in our lives, but if we let them get out of that place, they become dangerous and destructive. The main thrust of this book is to help you put the phone and electronic devices where they belong.

You are the head of the family, and time is precious. Do not let electronic devices and phones steal your family time. The best use of your time should be in talking and interacting with your children and instilling the right values in them. Nothing can substitute being present and engaging your children without any distractions. It is better to give your children 30 minutes of intentional focused time than hours of distracted and unengaged time.

A special note about driving

It is impossible to deceive your children; they watch what you do and follow it. If you are still texting and talking on the phone while driving and hoping that your children will not do the same when they start driving, you are in for a shock. How do you expect your children not to do what you are faithfully modeling before them? What makes you think that the child will follow a different path from the one that you have set before them?

Children do what they see, not what they are told! If you believe strongly about anything but do not act on it, you are disingenuous. Your children are extremely smart and have already figured that out. Each time you are lecturing them about the dangers of texting and answering phone calls while behind the wheel, all they're thinking is, "It is not that bad because daddy and mommy are always texting while driving. They are always talking on the phone while driving, and nothing bad has happened to them."

In short, because we see through pictures and eventually learn through pictures, what you demonstrate through your actions to your children is more powerful than any lecture you give them, especially when all you do is give instructions but fail to follow them yourself.

The future of your children depends on you setting the right example by doing what you want them to do when they become older. You must stop the bad habit of texting and taking phone calls while you are behind the wheel. If you want your children to turn off their phones when talking to you, it is your responsibility to show them how. Whatever you desire for your children, you must model it by your actions. Talk is cheap; you have to set the right example by adding the right actions to your words. There is nothing more powerful than being a person of integrity. In other words, your words and actions must line up. Now is the time to ensure that your talk about the phone, television, and other electronic devices lines up with your actions.

To set a good example, my wife and I have decided that receiving or making calls while driving when our children are in the car are not allowed, and we do everything to adhere to it.

This is one of the crucial things you as a parent will do for your children because of the pervasive nature of electronic devices in our modern-day life. Do not shy away from doing this. Take the bull by the horns. The earlier you start setting the example, the better.

Do not assume that the three-month-old baby sitting in the car seat is not watching, listening, and copying you. When it comes to driving and using electronic devices with kids in the car, you need a zero-tolerance policy and must implement it as soon as possible. You should not text and drive even if you do not have kids. (In some US states, it is actually against the law.) Never forget that to influence others, you need to set the right example. When you speak from experience and integrity, it has weight and will bring conviction and, eventually, change.

I hope you and your children will be safe, and you will set the right example for them to follow when they become adults so that they, too, will be safe and make others safe. You know how annoying it is when you come across those distracted drivers who are on their phones trying to do one thing or the other. When you raise your children to do the right thing, you are ensuring that our roads will have fewer distracted and dangerous motorists. Thank you for doing that.

Chapter 6:
The Myth

"In this media-drenched, multitasking, always-on age, many of us have forgotten how to unplug and immerse ourselves completely in the moment. We have forgotten how to slow down. Not surprisingly, this fast-forward culture is taking a toll on everything, from our diet and health to our work and the environment."
—Carl Honore

The case of Peter

Peter prides himself as somebody who has mastered multitasking because he usually checks his emails or eats lunch while on the phone. Most of his friends have brought to his attention that when he has food in his mouth and is talking over the phone, he sounds weird, not to mention impolite and unprofessional. This gentle suggestion from his friends to change his habits are not well received by Peter. He argues that he does not have time, and multitasking helps him to maximize his time. Even his wife has tried unsuccessfully to discourage him from talking on the phone when they are out on date nights and even when they are having dinner at home. He is always saying that he is busy and needs to take the calls. If he is not taking calls, he is keeping up with whatever is on Facebook, Twitter, and other social media platforms.

Then, things slowly started going downhill for Peter. His work was getting sloppy and he was turning in reports with glaring and avoidable mistakes. His manager brought this to his attention, and he promised to do better. Unfortunately, the distractions from his phone were taking a bigger toll on him until one day, he did the unthinkable. He had received some nude and unsolicited images on his email and he somehow forwarded the email to the entire company. He only realized what he had done after concerned colleagues started flooding his inbox with messages to tell him what he had done.

Peter was in shock and felt as if the ground opened up and swallowed him. There was no place for him to hide and no way to justify what had happened. His manager called him at the end of the day and explained to him that company policy does not support such behavior, and he had to fire him because this was not the first time that he had made such an error in judgment. He once forwarded a love note meant for his wife to the entire company because he was on the phone talking with somebody and composing the email at the same time. When he wanted to insert his wife's email, he grabbed the company email list instead and sent it to the entire company. To make matters worse, it had sexually explicit information in it. After this incident, he pleaded and promised to do better, but the myth of multitasking had a stronghold on him. It cost him his job. Some people are less fortunate.

The case of Susan

Susan always boasted to her friends that she is an expert in multitasking, especially when she was behind the wheel. Her commute to work was about 45 minutes, and she tried to maximize those 45 minutes to the best of abilities. It was not uncommon for her to be putting on her makeup, eating breakfast, texting, and driving all at the same time. She had done this so many times that it was "normal" to her. Each time the issue of texting while driving was brought up at work, she would watch the videos, complete the mandatory training, but refused to change her ways.

Susan would tell her colleagues and friends that nothing would happen to her because she had mastered the route from her house to work and had multitasked for so many years without a single accident or incident. She would, however, occasionally admit to some near misses. For example, one day, she was approaching the last stop light before the turn to her office when the car in front of her suddenly stopped. She was focused on doing the finishing touches on her makeup and did not know. What saved her was that she was not speeding and had enough distance between her and the other driver.

On another occasion, her phone rang on her way to work, while she was driving and doing her makeup. In the course of reaching out to get her phone, she pushed the coffee cup, spilled hot coffee on her lap, and had to be taken into the emergency room. In spite of all these, Susan felt that she was invincible and nothing bad would happen to her.

One fateful day, she was planning to go out for a date in the evening, and her mind was focused on her makeup, and she was doing everything to perfect it before meeting her date. She was talking on her phone and driving as usual. While finishing her makeup, one of the brushes fell. As she bent down to pick up the brush, the slight second slowed her car enough for it to be rammed from behind by a drunken driver. The force of the impact was so strong that she lost control of her car, moved out of her lane, and ran into another car. This second impact was deadly. Her car was smashed beyond recognition and she died on the spot. When the fire truck and first responders arrived at the scene, they had to use a hydraulic tool to get her broken body out of the car. Her phone was held tightly in one of her palms.

Be smarter

Talking on the phone and doing other things may appear to make sense, but in the long run, it will hurt you. Focus on one activity and wait until you are done to engage in another activity.

You heard about not texting while driving, but you still do it. Why are you risking your life and the lives of other motorists? Why can't the text wait? The only way you stop texting while driving is to stop texting while driving. Your life is more important than the text message you are about to send.

The lives of other motorists are important, and you should not get somebody hurt by running into their car or slowing down because you are distracted, causing somebody to hit you from behind.

Consider how irritated you are when you are driving and the driver in front of you is distracted and slowing down the traffic. When you are on your phone and slowing down because you are distracted, you infuriate other drivers and may cause an accident.

Stop texting while driving before you kill somebody or get killed. Your life is more important than a text message. Put away the phone and if possible, turn it off. Some phone providers have a feature on the phone that prevents you from placing or receiving calls when driving. Turn on the feature and do not override it when you are driving.

Common sense dictates that you should focus on driving when you are behind the wheel. Too many people have died because of road accidents, and some of them are directly related to phone usage while driving. Promise yourself that you are not going to be a statistic.

Multitasking is a myth. You may think that you have mastered multitasking, but it will eventually catch up with you, and you will make a mistake that can cost your life or that of other people.

As simple as this may sound, you actually get more done when you create time blocks for the different activities you have to do each day. There should be time set aside just to make phone calls and to text. Trying to do everything at the same time will make you less productive.

Try time blocking and move away from multitasking, especially regarding your phone use. You are going to experience firsthand its power and impact on your safety and productivity.

Chapter 7:
The Call

"I think that texting and driving is a 100% no-go. I think it should be banned everywhere because you cannot be focused on looking ahead, in the mirrors, being aware of what's around you, and to type on a small keyboard and a small screen." — Allan McNish

The call should not only wait, it MUST wait, especially if the call is not an emergency and you are not an emergency responder or dispatcher. Must you take that phone call when you are cruising at more than 70 miles per hour down the freeway? Must you take that phone call in a school zone? Is it really necessary to take that phone call or read that text while driving? Must you take the call while you are already in bed and ready to sleep? What is the phone doing in bed with you in the first place? Must you take the call while at the dinner table with your family or friends? Is it mandatory to stop what you are doing and respond each time your phone rings or a text message comes in? Must you answer the phone and check your text messages while on a date with your wife or fiancée? Why must you interrupt an important conversation just because you have been conditioned to answer every call or text that comes in?

Now is the time affirm that the call can wait! The text message can wait as well! It is not mandatory for you to respond immediately when your phone rings or when you are in the middle of something important.

The phone must wait when you are sleeping. I cannot count the number of times I have called somebody, and they woke up from sleep. When that happens, I usually apologize and ask them to go back to sleep. Then, I gently tell them what I do when I go to bed to not get disrupted myself: I turn off the phone and leave it in the living room or bathroom. There is no way my sleep will be interrupted by a phone call because the phone is off, and it is not even in my bedroom.

This may sound drastic, but the truth is that there is little I can do if my phone rings in the middle of the night because whoever is calling me is better off calling 911 or some other emergency response number, depending on where they are in the world. I have yet to miss some important appointment or deal because I do not sleep with my phone under my pillow.

The issue boils down to who is in charge. Is it you or your phone? If you are having difficulties staying away from your phone, you have a problem, and it is high time you dealt with it squarely. One sure way is to tell yourself that the call must wait. You are not at the mercy of phone calls and text messages and you are not under any obligation to answer them immediately as they come in. Always remember that you are not an emergency responder.

I was in class the other day and one of the students with one of those watches that have the capability to receive phones calls, dashed out while I was trying to explain a lab exercise. The simple reason was that a call had come in and that call had to be taken no matter what. Was it an emergency call? Could the call wait? It seemed the student did not ask these questions because he responded immediately when the call came in.

It is important to take a minute and ask yourself if the phone call can wait. In most cases, it can and nothing bad will happen. The world will not come to an end because you missed a phone call. Allowing the phone to take over your life is not a good idea.

When you are on your way home, and you know your husband or wife and even your children are eagerly waiting for you, make sure that you are not on the phone when you walk in. Whoever you are on the phone with is not as important as your husband or wife. The person may be your high school buddy, your best friend, boss, etc. If you walk into your house while on the phone, it is a sign that you are taking them for granted. Stop saying that your family would understand. Why not make whoever is on the phone understand that you're at home with your family?

The world is not passing you by

Many are under the illusion that checking their phone constantly throughout the day is an indication that they are engaging the world and staying on top of everything. In addition to keeping track of everything, they do not want the world to pass them by.

You are not missing anything, and the world is not passing you by. Stop worrying about it.

Pay attention, or you will get hurt

There are too many horror stories of cooking gone south because somebody left a pot on the stove while browsing Facebook or engaged in a phone conversation. Your entire house can even catch on fire if you allow yourself to be distracted. Paying attention and focusing on what you are doing is important and this will prevent accidents, injuries, and even death.

When you are at home and want to prepare food, it is time to put your phone away and focus on the task at hand. This does not mean that you cannot be preparing food and talking on the phone or browsing the internet. If you make this a habit, you are setting yourself up for a potential accident sooner or later. The wise thing to do is to block time for a specific task, and you would have significantly reduced or even eliminated the probability of having an accident as a result of being distracted.

Chapter 8:
The Password

"As soon as you start feeling like you can't trust the person and you need to check his phone or have his Facebook password or look through his messages, as soon as that trust barrier is broken, it's hard to keep a relationship going after that." —*Austin Butler*

I have been asked if it is OK for a husband and wife to know the passwords to each other's phones. This is an interesting and unfortunate question, to say the least. This may be an indication that there are trust issues in the relationship. Let me start with what we have in our home. My wife has the password to my phone and can access the phone anytime she wants. I also have the password to her phone and have access to it. This arrangement makes sense because if anything happens to me, God forbid, she will have access to the stuff that I have on my phone. Secondly, there is nothing that I am hiding from her, and she is not hiding anything from me. I am not afraid of her seeing the interactions that I have online with other people because I keep them honest and pure.

Purity to me is ensuring that each time I start any conversation with the opposite sex, I make it crystal clear that I am happily married and the father of five beautiful children, and I do not play any games. There is zero room for flirting and ungodly exchanges.

Some may disagree with this approach, but it is reckless to scoop hot coals with your bare hands and think that your hands will not get hurt. Your marriage is sacred and must be protected at all times. You are the gatekeeper and should guard against anything that will threaten the purity of your marriage. If you believe that flirting once in a while is OK, sooner or later, you will act on the feelings and emotions that have been building.

This is not an attempt to force my beliefs on anybody, but you shall know the truth, and the truth will set you free. If you are struggling with the tendency to be flirtatious with men or women and straying into pornographic sites, it is time for you to break free from this bondage. Do not open the door for the enemy to get in and destroy your marriage. This is because your marriage is more important than having a flirtatious conversation or chat with some other person.

Share your password

Everything written in this book is not a commandment, and you have the right not to follow any of it. All I am doing is presenting the information and the consequences for not taming your phone and doing what is right for you, your family and relationships. If you are not already sharing your passwords, now is the time to go ahead and do it. When you do it, your marriage will definitely have a stronger foundation, and the hedge of protection around it will be stronger. You have eliminated the possibility of having skeletons in your closet and have nipped many destructive tendencies that may creep in directly from the bud.

You may say, "I have a company phone and the company policy stipulates that I do not share my password with anybody." You are correct under these circumstances, but you may need a second phone to do your personal affairs. In that case, you may share the password for that. By the way, if you are using a company phone, it is prudent to use it strictly for company business, not your personal stuff. While using the company phone, it is not a good idea to visit pornographic sites and flirt with other people as well.

What are you hiding?

If you cannot share your password with your spouse, what are you hiding from each other? Is it a time bomb that will explode and destroy your marriage? Healthy relationships do all to defuse time bombs because they can become deadly if not eliminated. For now, it may appear as if there is nothing happening, but one day, you will deeply regret putting skeletons in your closet.

If you want to deepen the trust in your marriage, then open up and let each other have access to each other. This sounds counterintuitive, but marriage makes the two one, not two. Some of the challenges couples are facing in their marriages can be attributed to the lack of transparency, which leads to the erosion of trust. It is crucial to understand that trust is the bedrock of any healthy relationship. Without trust, it is impossible to build a healthy and lasting marriage.

You may be protesting that sharing your passwords is not necessary and it will be akin to opening a can of worms or Pandora's Box. If you feel that we should allow sleeping dogs to lie because we risk causing a problem where there is none, I beg to differ. The fact that you feel like this is because there is something that you are hiding and what you are hiding will eventually be exposed. This may happen at a time that you are not ready, and it may not end well.

Now is the time to stop all the suspicions that are brewing in your relationship and restore trust and confidence in each other. According to the Bible, "True love drives away all fears." If fear is preventing you from trusting your husband or wife, it is time to unleash love to drive away that fear and bring both of you closer and your relationship deeper.

If you insist that there is no point in sharing your passwords, then you must determine if you are happy with the present situation of your marriage. If you are doing fine, then you make the judgment call and do what you believe is the best course of action for your marriage.

Chapter 9:
The Proper Place

"I think technology is us, not something we invented. I think we are more psychic now because we have cell phones and you can look and see who's calling you. When people start seeing technology as us, as humanity, our whole idea of what existence is, is going to shift." ——*Ryan Trecartin*

This is the electronic age, and more and more devices are flooding the already saturated marketplace and competing for our time and attention. Concentrating on a single task is becoming more and more difficult with each passing day. Therefore, each individual needs to learn how to put all electronic devices in their proper place to mitigate their impact on the quality of our relationships.

Electronic devices have been created to serve us, not the other way around. It is a disaster when what was made to serve has become the master. We are supposed to be controlling when, where, and why we use our phones and other electronic devices. It becomes a serious problem when we let the devices take over our lives. The consequences are totally undeniable, and it is crucial that an intervention plan be put in place.

It is never too late to do the right thing. And in this case, it is to put your phone and electronic devices in their proper place. You may be saying that you do not have any problem with your phone or electronic devices. Let us see:

- Do you have a hard time sitting through a meeting without checking your phone?
- Are you always checking your phone to see what the last trending issue is?
- Can you go for a day without checking your phone?
- When on vacation, do you find it difficult to totally unplug, relax, and enjoy your time off ?
- Is your wife complaining that you are spending too much time on your phone?
- Is your husband concerned about the amount of time you spend on the phone?
- Do you go to bed with your phone?
- Do you answer every call that comes in no matter what you are doing?
- Do you text while driving?
- Have other people brought to your attention that your phone is a distraction?
- Do you find it difficult to concentrate at work because you have to constantly check your phone and go on social media?
- Do you think you have a phone addiction?
- When people bring to your attention that you are spending too much time on the phone, do you argue and justify it?

- Are you fond of dropping everything and responding to text messages that come in when you are in the middle of something?
- Do you get a "high" from using your phone and other electronic devices?
- Do you feel helpless when it comes to controlling your phone usage?
- Is the quality of your work negatively impacted because you are on the phone most of the time?
- Do you believe that multitasking, especially being on your phone and doing many other things, is efficient and effective?
- Is your phone the first thing you reach for when you get out of bed?
- Do you feel guilty about using your phone because you are spending a lot of time on it when it could be spent on something else?
- Do you panic when you cannot find your phone?
- Has your phone become part of your life and you feel incomplete without it?
- Do you miss meals and neglect other important bodily functions because you are using your phone?
- Do you believe that you have mastered texting and driving, and nothing can go wrong while you are doing so?
- Do you feel a part of you is missing when your phone is not with you?
- Is your phone the last thing you look at before going to bed?
- Are you struggling to concentrate on the task at hand because you are constantly checking your phone and the social media feed?

- Do you feel your phone or electronic devices have taken over your life?
- Do you panic when your wife or husband picks up your phone?
- Do you find it impossible to be without your phone?
- Do you text at stoplights?
- Have you been honked by other drivers because your phone was distracting you?

If you answered yes to any of these questions, then it is time for you to ensure that the phone and other electronic devices are put in their proper place. This is not going to be an easy process, and it will demand some changes on your part.

Admit that you have a problem

Many people would rather blame their phones than their lack of self- control. It is not strange to hear statements like, "I can't help it! I can't function without my phone. I must keep up with what is happening." Some are honest enough to say, "I am addicted to my phone, and it has become my life."

To break free, you must admit the dependency on your phone and take personal responsibility for the bad habits that you cultivated over the years. Why is turning off your phone more difficult than turning it on? What is it about that phone that you are willing to die for? Texting while driving is one of the most irresponsible, foolish, and reckless things to do.

Yet, thousands of people are texting while driving right now. Why? What in the world are they thinking? What is cool about jeopardizing your life and those of others because that text message cannot wait?

If you are texting while driving, it is an indication that you have a serious problem. It does not matter for how many years you have done it successfully. Now is the time to admit and ask for help. The good news is that help is available.

Admit that you need help

When you accept that you have a problem, the next step is to accept that you need help. If you do not identify the problem and ask for help, you will not solve it. In this case, we are talking about how much influence your phone and other electronic devices are having on your life. You have lost control of your life because of these devices and now is the time to own up to it and ask for help.

The help that you need is available, but it is 100% dependent on you. You are the owner of your phone, and it is your responsibility to put the phone in its proper place. Nobody is going to do this for you.

Now that you have admitted that you have a problem and is seeking help, there is hope for you. If you were not looking for help, you would not be reading this book.

Admit the need for change

It is not enough to admit that you have a problem and ask for help. You must admit the need to change. It has been said that "Insanity is doing the same thing and expecting a different outcome."

Somebody came to you and said they have planted corn but are expecting to harvest soybeans. Then, the person proceeds to say that you should sign a contract for them to supply soybeans when the crops are harvested. What will you tell this farmer?

Anybody in their right mind will not sign the contract and will immediately and not-so-politely show this unscrupulous farmer the door. This illustration sounds absurd, but many people behave like that. They refuse to make any changes yet expect a different outcome. How is this possible?

If you do not admit the need for change, it will be impossible for you to change. This may sound too simplistic, but it is a necessary step. Failure to admit the need for change will prevent you from seeking change and taking the necessary actions that will bring the much- needed change.

People are usually hesitant to admit the need for change because they think it is an admission that they are weak. Admitting that you need to change is a sign of strength, not weakness. Those who continue on the path of destruction and refuse to change are weak; the strong recognize that without change, they will not get a different outcome.

The phone and other electronic devices may be the reason the quality of your relationships have suffered. Therefore, the prudent thing to do is to make up your mind and do all that is necessary for you to change the way things are at the moment. Nobody is going to do this for you. Now is the time for you to ACT!

Take action

You are not going to continue life as usual, and this is your opportunity to make some changes. Of what use is all this information if you are not willing to act on it? It does not matter how much you know — without action, nothing will change.

You may have the best intentions, but if you do not act, your intentions mean nothing. I have two neighbors: one who does not like immigrants because I am the only immigrant in my neighborhood, and another neighbor who always says that he likes immigrants. One day, I was out of the house and a burglar was trying to break into my house. The neighbor who does not like immigrants called 911 and the police came and intervened. The other neighbor who always said he loves immigrants saw the burglar but did nothing. Who is the good neighbor in this situation?

The answer is pretty obvious. The other neighbor had good intentions and even professed them, but those intentions meant nothing because he did not act on them. Action is what separates the authentic from the fake. Without concrete action, your good and noble intentions mean nothing.

How many times have you promised to stop texting while driving? You feel guilty each time you text while driving and have vowed to stop this terrible habit.

One way to get the inspiration and motivation that you need to make the necessary changes is to count the cost that is associated with your actions. Ask yourself the following questions:

- Is spending time on your phone more important than your marriage?
- Have you considered the cost of a divorce if you continue on this trajectory?
- Is it worth losing your job because you are distracted by your phone and lack concentration? Have you considered the cost of sitting in meetings and missing out on important decisions because your phone distracted you?
- Is it worth it to kill others or risk being killed because you are texting while driving?

- Have you considered the negative health effects because your phone is interfering with the quality of your sleep?
- Do you really want to reduce your lifespan because of an electronic device?

While I am talking about the cost of using electronic devices and the detrimental impact this has on our health, relationships, finances, etc., I will draw your attention to what I have observed firsthand in the classroom.

When drafting my syllabus at the beginning of each semester, I clearly state on it that phones and other electronic devices should not be turned on in class during lectures. The reason I do it is thatmultitasking is a myth, and it is impossible to concentrate and listen to music, watch YouTube videos or browse the internet at the same time. Some students take action and put away their phones, but others ignore the advice and put on earphones during lectures. While the rest of the class is answering questions and interacting with me, other students are in their own world. They are physically in class but somewhere else emotionally and mentally. I know these students are not there because they don't follow simple instructions concerning exercises and assignments. When I teach, a few clues about what may be expected in the test are sprinkled throughout the lecture and emphasis is made for the students to pay close attention. The students who are on their electronics think they are paying attention but are betrayed when testing time comes.

Chapter 10:
The One in Charge

"Every time there's a new tool, whether it's the Internet or cell phones or anything else, all these things can be used for good or evil. Technology is neutral; it depends on how it's used."
—*Rick Smolan*

Who is in charge: you or your phone? This should not be asked, but I must because it appears that the phone is in charge. Many people are at the mercy of these devices. Like any tyrant who has gained total control, these devices are merciless and do not care about those that have been enslaved by them.

Right now, it is easy for many to say that they are in charge. Their stand is based on their understanding that an object cannot be in charge. They are the ones who bought the phone and they decide when to turn it on, when to charge it, and when to turn it off. The phone cannot carry itself around and depends totally on its owner to pick it up, dial it, text or browse the Internet, etc. Without the owner, the phone is helpless. There is completely nothing the phone can do on its own. The owner decides when to discard the phone and get a new one.

Those who hold this view are correct. But why are we having a phone and electronic device problem then? The answer is simple, "Action speaks louder than words." What you think, desire, and talk about means nothing if you act contrary to it. If you are still texting while driving and claiming that you are in charge, you are deceiving yourself. The true boss is your phone.

If you are having a hard time focusing on a task because you have to constantly check your phone and keep up with incoming texts, calls, news, trending events, etc., you are not in charge — your phone is.

If you get into a panic attack because you cannot find your phone and start feeling as if part of your body is gone, you are not in charge — your phone is.

Denying it and pretending that you are in charge will not set you free. If you are truly in charge, you will do what the owner and master of an object will do: turn off the phone when driving. When you are involved in an important task, you turn off the phone or put it away.

The truth is that you are in charge and should not allow feelings of failure and inadequacy to prevent you from being the boss that you already are. Take charge and let your actions speak louder than your words. If you think you believe that texting while driving is bad, yet you keep doing it, you do not believe that it is bad. If you think that being on the phone all the time is destroying your relationships, but keep doing it, you do not believe that the phone is destroying your relationships.

Now is the time to show your phone and electronic devices who is truly in charge. Do it by turning off the devices when your visitors come to visit you. When you are driving, when at work, when attending meetings, when you visit other people, show them respect by turning off your phone.

The phone has its proper place, and you should ensure that it occupies that place. You have to do this because you are the one in charge. Stop saying that you cannot help it, or it is impossible to function without the phone. The truth of the matter is that you will do great without it because it is just a tool. How you feel about the phone should not determine how you treat it.

Hopefully, by now, you are convinced that the phone needs to obey you and not the other way around. Many people may say, "How dare you to suggest that my phone is controlling my life! Have you forgotten that I am the one who picks up the phone and turn it on and can turn it off when I want to?"

The issue here is not about picking up the phone and turning it on or off. It is about when and where you pick it up and turn it on and off. If you say you are in charge, then stop browsing the Internet and fidgeting with your phone during meetings and when you have guests over or are visiting someone. Can you back up your words with action?

Chapter 11:
The Parent

"These days, children can text on their cell phone all night long, and no one else is seeing that phone. You don't know who is calling that child." ——*Kamala Harris*

Parents desire and wish that their children do well in all aspects of their lives. Many make great sacrifices and go to great lengths to make this happen. In short, they love their children and this love inspires and motivates them to accomplish great things on behalf of their children.

The backdrop of what I am about to discuss is the understanding that no parent will knowingly harm their child. Some of it may be hard to accept, but it has to be said because it is crucial.

Do not give phones to young children

Before you throw this book away because I am advocating that you should not give a phone to a young child, I would like you to hear me out. This suggestion may make sense to you, but the pressure to fit in is stronger than doing what is right for you and your child.

First and foremost, why do parents give phones to young children? There are many justifications. The one that stands out the most is that of staying in contact with their children. While it is crucial for parents to stay in touch with their children, the pros and cons of giving phones to young children have to be weighed carefully. Unfortunately, the drawback for young children having phones is immense and parents should not set up their children for unnecessary distractions.

I have seen too many students struggling to pay attention in class because of their phones. Many of these students find it almost impossible to stay away from their phones. Some said, "The phone keeps me awake." It is unfortunate that these devices are taking a toll on their academic performance. Most of them got their phones when they were young and have gotten used to having them. The phone is a powerful device and has a lot of potential, but it can become destructive if not used at the right time.

There is great potential for abuse and other people can be harmed as a result of this abuse. Cyber bullying is becoming more rampant, and some children have committed suicide as a result of being bullied by other children online. Why would you buy a phone and give it to your child if you knew that the phone was going to cause their death? No parent in their right mind will do this. But it is happening more than we think.

A few months ago, I was listening to the radio about the parents of a young girl who committed suicide after binge-watching a show on Netflix that glorified suicide. What drew my attention to the story is the fact that this young girl was watching the show on her phone in her room without the knowledge of her parents. Her parents were only able to reconstruct what happened after her death. This unfortunate incident would have been avoided if more parental control of the use of electronic devices was implemented. This is not playing the blame game here. The parents wished they had done more, but it was too late. Their advice to all parents is to monitor what their children are doing on their devices.

You can completely eliminate the need to monitor by not providing the phone in the first place. This solves the problem at the root. If you must give the phone to your child, then you will have to set some strict rules and ensure that your child follows them. Many children do not sleep well these days because they are on their phones chatting with their friends and exchanging pictures and images that you the parent will be shocked if you saw them. There are too many sad stories of phone usage gone wrong that we do not have room to write about them here.

To say NO to the demands of your children for a phone or other electronic device is not easy, but you do it because you love them enough and it is your responsibility to protect them. We have five children, and none of them has a phone. The oldest is a junior in high school and this has not impacted his quality of life in any way. For now, when he is in class, there is no worry about him being distracted.

No electronic devices in the rooms

If you must give a phone to your children, then you have to follow these basic suggestions. Otherwise, you will lead your child into temptation. I have already said that the ideal situation is for the child not to have any phone until they are old enough to learn how to be in control and not have the device controlling them, as is happening with many kids these days.

Let the electronic devices be placed in a central area where the children will not have access to them when it is bedtime. Did I hear you ask, "What about the privacy of the children?" Privacy? Do you care about the privacy of your children more than their lives? You may want to ask the parents of the 14-year-old who binge-watched *13 Reasons Why* on her phone in her room and killed herself. According to them, her death was caused by the content she watched because it glorified suicide and provided ways to carry it out. This unfortunate girl went ahead and implemented one of the methods that were depicted in the show.

Giving electronic devices to your children and refusing to monitor and control their usage is irresponsible, to say the least. This may not make sense to you but ask the parent of the woman who went out with her young son for a function and got embarrassed by him. When this lady arrived the party, all the children were placed in a separate room for the adults to have fun. Her son took his iPad and decided to introduce all the other children to what adults do behind closed doors. Unknown to this woman, her son, who was younger than 10 years old, had been watching pornography on his iPad and thought it was a brilliant idea to share it with other children. According to his mother, he was too young for such content, and there was no reason to suspect that he was consuming such content. Can you imagine her embarrassment and shock when the parents of the other children brought this to her attention?

One of the parents had gone into the room where the kids were supposed to be playing and interacting with each other and was surprised when all of them were clustered in one corner. When she got closer to them, she realized that they were all glued to the iPad screen. This made her even more curious, and she immediately asked them to hand over the device to her. She could not believe the trash this young child was watching, including her own. What was transpiring did not sit well with her at, and she immediately went and brought it to the mother of the little boy at the center of all this drama. She was so ashamed and perplexed that she took her son and left the party immediately.

Do you want to dismiss this under the pretext that "kids will be kids?" It seems you have forgotten the damage watching adult content will have on these children and how it will negatively impact their sexual life in the future. If something like this does not trouble you and you think that it is OK for your child to consume pornography at a tender age, you are seriously mistaken.

You must also consider cyber bullying and the ramification that goes with it. Some children have committed suicide because their "friends" took compromising images of them and shared them with other people. If you have not heard of sex texting, maybe that should trouble you. Some of these teenagers get excited and send nude pictures to friends, believing that they will keep their word and not share the pictures. Those sending the pictures fail to understand that as soon as you click the Send button, whatever you sent is completely out of your control and can end of up in places you may not be very proud of. Why risk it? Limit the amount of time your children spend on their phones when they are at home. It is a wise idea to also limit the amount of time your children spend on their electronic devices just playing games.

Turn off the TV

I am going to say something controversial and I will allow the chips to fall where they may. Allowing the TV to run perpetually at home is a bad idea. We become what we meditate upon and what we meditate upon gets into our minds through what we watch, listen, and read. Therefore, we must be extremely careful with the information that we allow to get into our minds. Unfortunately, many people do not care. They may say they don't, but their actions betray them. We are constantly being bombarded by so much negative information that it does not make sense to continue bringing them it into your living room.

How many times do you feel excited, inspired and motivated after watching the news on TV? The truth is that all this negative information is depressing and makes you discouraged with life, in general. It is not easy to shut out all negative information from getting to us, but we must do all within our power to keep this information out.

This battle starts with turning off the TV that you have in your living room. Yes, the TV has to be turned off and remain off as much as possible. We do not turn on the TV in our home during the week because our children are of school age and have to do their homework and study. These two activities take precedence over everything else, including watching TV. Because our children do not watch TV, we the adults in the house do not watch the TV as well. This may sound draconian to some people, but it is the best thing for our children, and they are doing great.

Do not expect your children to turn off the TV if you do not lead the way. It is your responsibility as the parent to set the boundaries and help your children establish the right habits. The sooner you start, the better for you and your children. This is because young children are easier to train than older ones. We have a 17-year-old, and he was raised in this atmosphere and has no problem at all. When it is Friday afternoon, the TV is turned on, then on Sunday evening it is watched. In some homes, the TV is running most of the time, whether somebody is watching it or not. This is not a good practice and should be discouraged.

It is up to you as the parent to set the rules in your home and ensure that your children are obeying them. If you educate them about the perils of electronic devices and model the right habits before them, you would have done an excellent investment that will pay off big time in the future.

Chapter 12:
The Options

"Want of foresight, unwillingness to act when action would be simple and effective, lack of clear thinking, confusion of counsel until the emergency comes, until self-preservation strikes its jarring gong — these are the features which constitute the endless repetition of history." —*Winston Churchill*

Of what use is the information in a book if the book is not read and no action is taken? Why do you read a book if you are not willing to apply the message in the book? How can you continue on the trajectory you are currently on, yet expect to land somewhere else? When a captain gets into a ship, he checks the course. If not, the ship, no matter how sophisticated and equipped it is, will not arrive at the destination because it has not been placed on the right course.

You have two options before you: do nothing and continue on the path you are on right now or make the much-needed changes in the way you interact with your phone and other electronic devices.

Do nothing

We started by saying that this issue is some sort of an elephant in the room because many people do not like to talk about it. Although people are not talking about it, they wish the issue can be discussed openly. Nobody likes to be ignored. If you do, then you are one of the few. You may be saying that, "Being on the phone while others are in the room with you is not the same as ignoring them."

Are you telling me that multitasking in this manner is efficient and effective? Can you be an active listener while on your phone texting or watching some video on YouTube? You must be a superhuman to do this. Even if you could multitask effectively, how do you think those you are interacting with are perceiving you? There is nothing more annoying than talking to somebody and all they care about is fidgeting with their phone or some electronic device.

If you get together with other people and they are engaging in this bad behavior of gluing themselves to their phones, you should not join them. The reason is simple: if you do not smoke nor drink alcohol, you will not necessarily start drinking because you went to visit a friend who was smoking or drinking. The reason for not smoking should be strong enough to prevent you from engaging in this destructive behavior. In other words, just because other people are doing something is not an excuse for you to engage in it. You must have heard that you should "be the change you want."

Do not forget that not doing anything implies that nothing will change in your life as well. You will continue to ignore your guest at your peril. You will attend meetings and miss out because you are distracted. There is a probability that if you are texting while driving, you may get killed or kill somebody. As harsh as this may sound, it has to be brought to your attention.

Act

I have often said that it is self-deceit to say that you know something but take no action. If you say you know smoking is bad for you, yet you continue smoking, the truth is that you only have head knowledge about smoking, but do not really know. When you "know", it produces results. No wonder the Bible uses the word "know" to describe a sexual relationship between a man and a woman. Knowing is intimate and involves action. Without any action, you do not know. Period. It does not matter if you insist on the contrary. Nobody in their right mind will jump over a cliff if they know that jumping will kill them. The only explanation is if this particular individual wants to commit suicide, then their action will make sense.

If you decide to take action after everything you have read in this book and other resources, you are on the right path. This is a wise and smart thing to do. Action is what will set you apart and open a new frontier and great possibilities for you. The distraction from phones and electronic devices is huge. You are going to save so much time that you will be surprised by how much you have been spending. Time is money, and it is something that many people have not mastered. The more control you have over your time, the more productive you are going to be.

Unfortunately, modern electronic devices are a big thief of time. Many people waste time looking at pictures on Facebook and other social media platforms without any purpose. All they do is to jump from one platform to the other, making comments that are baseless.

You have to be intentional on how you use your electronic devices; if not, you will not maximize your time. Some do not consider their time as precious. No wonder they squander it each day without thought. You know better.

Now that you are done reading this book, if you do not put what you have learned into action, you just wasted your time. But if you do, your investment is going to pay off. The time that you will be freed from the addiction to your phone and electronic devices will be used for more productive activities. Your relationships are going to get better because you are paying attention and connecting as you should.

Chapter 13:
The Most Important
Thing

"Wonder blasts the soul - that is, the spiritual - and the skeleton, the body - the material. Wonder interprets life through the eyes of eternity while enjoying the moment, but never lets the moment's revision exhaust the eternal." —*Ravi Zacharias*

Before you continue, I want to say congratulations! You have done what many people do not. Most people start books and never finish reading them. Yet, you persevered, and now you are here. There is nothing more important than being a child of God. I will be wicked if I do not share this truth with you. It is one of the most important things that you will ever do. It is more important than taking care of your physical body because your body will eventually decay.

I do not know where you are in your own spiritual journey. No matter where you are, I strongly encourage you to read this chapter and make sure that you put things right with God. You are being offered an opportunity to have God come and live in you. This should excite you more than having the perfect body.

When our Lord Jesus Christ says something, it is important that we take it seriously. Here is one of the most important Bible verses that puts everything in perspective:

For what profit is it to a man if he gains the whole world, and loses his own soul? Or what will a man give in exchange for his soul? Matthew 16:26 (NKJV)

Here, Jesus Christ is asking a profound question that everybody must answer. You cannot afford to keep going through life without answering these questions, because how your life ends will determine the answer to these questions. It is interesting that the body is not mentioned in the verse. But the soul is what is front and center because the body will finally die and decay, but the soul is going to live forever.

There is nothing more important than your soul, and you should take this seriously. While there is nothing wrong in being successful in this life, if you neglect what is more important, you are going to have all eternity to regret it.

The major assumption throughout this book is that you are a believer in the Lord Jesus Christ. This implies that you have given your life to him and accepted him as your Lord and savior. In addition to being born again, you are walking daily with the Lord and bearing the fruit of the Holy Spirit.

Having an eternal perspective is the ultimate because, at the end of the day, it is eternal that matters. People have looked for the foundation of youth over the ages, and there is a lot of research right now to understand aging and how to reverse it. Even if we were to find the fountain of youth and drink from it so that we remain young forever, life on earth will still have a lot of changes for us. This also implies that after reversing aging and making sure that we remain young here on earth we are still going to face other challenges because we are living in a fallen world with many different problems.

I say all this to emphasize the importance of looking forward to our true and final home, where we will be with our Heavenly Father forever and ever. While life on earth is great, life in heaven is going to be greater and more fulfilling. This is something that all God's children have to look forward to.

But if you are not yet a child of God, here is your opportunity for you to learn how to become a child of God. You cannot afford to neglect this crucial issue or put it off for another day. Let this be a sign that it is time for you to make things right with God.

Life does not end when you die. There is an afterlife, and I am going to use this opportunity to tell you about it. Talking about the afterlife is not an indirect way for you to disengage with the present life, but a motivation for you to do make the most of your time on earth. While there are many arguments about which roads led to God and which God is true, I am not going to dwell on these issues. The reason being is that there is not enough room for us to do a comparative study of the world religions.

That said, it is important to note that while popular culture classifies Christianity as a religion and tries to compare it to other religions, the truth is that Christianity is not a religion. If religion is mankind trying their best to reach out to God and please Him, Christianity is the exact opposite. God is the person who is reaching out to mankind and doing all to redeem us. To enjoy this redemption that God is offering, you must follow instructions.

I am writing this with the assumption that you have been reconciled with God and have a relationship with him. If you do not yet have a relationship with God, I am going to give you the opportunity here to take care of that. This is one of the most important decisions you will ever make and should not take it lightly. I do not want you to allow the failures of other believers that you might have interacted with to prevent you from getting into a personal relationship with your heavenly Father. He has been waiting for you to come home and be reunited with Him.

Here is your opportunity to come home to the fullness of life and abundant life. All that you need and desire is in God, and you will never be forsaken or abandoned.

Let me start by asking you the following question: *do you have a personal relationship with Jesus Christ?* This question is being asked because although all roads lead to Rome, not all roads lead to the God of the Bible. Jesus Christ, who is God Incarnate, made some exclusive claims when He said,

"Jesus answered, "I am the way and the truth and the life. No one comes to the Father except through me." John 14:6 (NIV)

This is a bold claim, and Jesus Christ died for standing up for this. He is simply saying that if you want a relationship with the God of the Bible, who is also the Creator of heaven and earth, you must pass through Him. If you are not a yet a follower of Jesus Christ, here is your opportunity to do so. I suggest this because it is going to get you connected to the source of all things. You will become spiritually alive and will live forever in the presence of God. Raising your child with the fear of God is the best thing you can do for you and your child.

We all have sinned

In other words, we cannot meet God's perfect standard, no matter how hard we try. Have you tried on your own to be good and realized many times how you do not measure up? Do you struggle with a void in your heart that nothing has been able to fill, no matter how hard you have tried? Are you comparing yourself to others and feeling that you are good because you are better than other people? If you answered yes to any these questions, you need to understand that all of us have sinned, just as the following scriptures clearly spell out.

"For all have sinned and come short of the glory of God." Romans 3:23

"For there is not a just man upon earth, that doeth good, and sinneth not." Ecclesiastes 7:20

"But we are all as an unclean thing, and all our righteousnesses are as filthy rags, and we all do fade as a leaf; and our iniquities, like the wind, have taken us away." Isaiah 64:6

"As it is written, there is none righteous, no, not one." Romans 3:10

"For whosoever shall keep the whole law, and yet offend in one point, he is guilty of all." James 2:10

"If we say that we have no sin, we deceive ourselves, and the truth is not in us." 1 John 1:8

We have all sinned and need God's forgiveness. This is the place to start. When you acknowledge this, then you will be able to receive God's free forgiveness and salvation.

The devastating consequences of sin

You may be wondering why sin is such a bad thing and why we are making such a big deal about it. Everybody, including you, should be concerned about the consequences of sin because, according to the following verse, sin has a wage, and that wage is death.

> *For the wages of sin is death, but the free gift of God is eternal life in Christ Jesus, our Lord. Romans 6:23 ESV*

> *Therefore, just as sin came into the world through one man, and death through sin, and so death spread to all men because all sinned. Romans 5:12 ESV*

> *But as for the cowardly, the faithless, the detestable, as for murderers, the sexually immoral, sorcerers, idolaters, and all liars, their portion will be in the lake that burns with fire and sulfur, which is the second death. Revelation 21:8 ESV*

This death is both physical and spiritual. Sin can cause us to die in this life, and if we die in sin, we will be separated from God forever. You do not want this to happen to you and your child or children. You want to be able to live forever in the presence of God. This is why the second crucial thing to think about is the wages of sin.

Ask God to forgive our sins

The good news is that God has already made provision to forgive our sins and is ready and willing to forgive us all our sins. As you will soon discover, God has already made the first move.

"For God so loved the world, that he gave his only begotten Son, that whosoever believeth in him should not perish, but have everlasting life." John 3:16

"Jesus said unto her, I am the resurrection, and the life: he that believeth in me, though he were dead, yet shall he live: And whosoever liveth and believeth in me shall never die. Believest thou this?" John 11:25-26

"And they said, Believe on the Lord Jesus Christ, and thou shalt be saved, and thy house." Acts 16:31

"That if thou shalt confess with thy mouth the Lord Jesus, and shalt believe in thine heart that God hath raised him from the dead, thou shalt be saved. {10} For with the heart man believeth unto righteousness; and with the mouth confession is made unto salvation." Romans 10:9-10

"Whosoever believeth that Jesus is the Christ is born of God: and every one that loveth him that begat loveth him also that is begotten of him." 1 John 5:1

Now that you have confessed and asked Jesus to forgive your sins, your sins have been forgiven and will be remembered no more.

Invite Jesus into your heart

Now is your opportunity to surrender your life to Jesus and invite Him to come into your heart. Jesus will never force himself on anyone. He is outside, according to the following scripture, knocking and waiting for you to invite Him to come in.

> *"Behold, I stand at the door, and knock: if any man hear my voice, and open the door, I will come in to him, and will sup with him, and he with me." Revelation 3:20*

> *"But as many as received him, to them gave he power to become the sons of God, even to them that believe on his name:" John 1:12*

> *"And because ye are sons, God hath sent forth the Spirit of his Son into your hearts, crying, Abba, Father." Galatians 4:6*

> *"That Christ may dwell in your hearts by faith; that ye, being rooted and grounded in love," Ephesians 3:17*

Jesus Christ is waiting for you to invite Him to come in and you can do that by praying and asking Him to do so. Use your own words to talk to Him or The Sinners Prayer by John Barnett.

The following prayer expresses the desire to transfer trust to Christ alone for eternal salvation. If its words speak of your own heart's desire, praying them can be the link that will connect you to God.

Dear God, I know that I am a sinner and there is nothing that I can do to save myself. I confess my complete helplessness to forgive my own sin or to work my way to heaven. At this moment I trust Christ alone as the One who bore my sin when He died on the cross. I believe that He did all that will ever be necessary for me to stand in your holy presence. I thank you that Christ was raised from the dead as a guarantee of my own resurrection. As best as I can, I now transfer my trust to Him. I am grateful that He has promised to receive me despite my many sins and failures. Father, I take you at your word. I thank you that I can face death now that you are my Savior. Thank you for the assurance that you will walk with me through the deep valley. Thank you for hearing this prayer. In Jesus' Name. Amen.

Praise God! Hallelujah! If you just said this prayer, I am super excited for you and want to use this opportunity to welcome you into the kingdom of God and God's family. This is one of the most important decisions you will ever make because it has eternal consequences. You are now a newborn baby in Christ and need spiritual nourishment to grow in your faith. If you need more information on what to do next, send an email.

It is extremely important that you understand the crucial nature of this decision you have just made. I want to highlight the fact that the focus has not been for you to join a religion or to become religious. Religion is a man seeking to please God. But here we have presented a picture of God seeking man. God loved the entire world, then gave His son to pay the penalty for our sins. This point is being made so that you understand that you are being called into a personal relationship with Jesus and not just some religious observances. While church membership is important, it is more important that you establish a strong and vibrant relationship with Jesus Christ.

(This entire plan of salvation has been borrowed from my material in other works I have written with little modifications).

About the Author

Dr. Eric Tangumonkem is a geoscientist, author, speaker, coach, professor, and an entrepreneur. He was born and raised in Cameroon, Africa. As a young adult, he migrated to the United States of America. He has a Doctorate degree in Geosciences from the University of Texas at Dallas and is a professor at Missional University, Embry Riddle, and West Hills College.

As President of IEM Approach, a premier personal growth and leadership development company, Dr. Tangumonkem's mission is to inspire, equip, and motivate people from all walks of life to discover God's potential in them live it, and maximize their giftedness. To do this, the growth and development of the body, mind, and spirit MUST be in synergy. He has published several books and resources on personal growth and development and conducts public workshops, coaching, and custom training programs for companies and organizations worldwide.

If you want to invite Dr. Tangumonkem to come and speak at your event, please call 317-975-0806 or email eternalkingdom101@gmail. com.

You can also follow him on social media Twitter: @DrTangumonkem
Facebook: drtangumonkem
Email: dr.tangumonkem@gmail.com

Other Resources by the Author

Why I Refused to Become an Illegal Alien: Navigating the Complexities of the American Immigration System

When it comes to the problem of illegal immigration, divisive rhetoric has shut out the voice of reason and common sense. Polarization has resulted in two extreme views--either open the borders wide and allow the free movement of people and goods, or close the borders and prevent people from coming in. The solution is somewhere in the middle . . . if we are willing to listen to one another. Why I Refused to Become an Illegal Alien chronicles the long and arduous journey of one man who immigrated legally and believes that the cost of allowing America's present immigration crisis to remain unresolved is too high. Drawing upon his deep Judeo- Christian roots, this newly-naturalized US citizen sets forth Bible-based solutions that emphasize the need to be our brother's keeper--to show love, mercy, and compassion and at the same time be fair and just.

Make Yourself at Home: An Immigrant's Guide to Settling in America

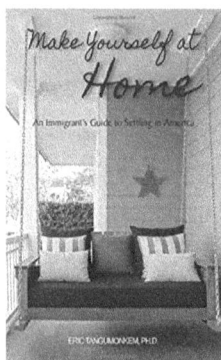

We live in a fallen world plagued by political unrest, conflicts, and wars. These factors, coupled with the desire for a better life, compel people to move to other areas—even across continents and oceans. Immigration brings people face to face with diverse cultures, and wherever diverse cultures meet, either there is immense personal growth, or things can go south quickly. The strategies introduced in this book are for immigrants who are new to the United States of America, but they are applicable to anyone who migrates within or outside of a country. Make Yourself at Home is a valuable resource for helping immigrants avoid the pitfalls experienced by those who have gone before them. Author Eric Tangumonkem, himself an immigrant and naturalized American citizen, presents practical assimilation strategies for education, money, home life, community, and health that, if followed, will position immigrants to excel in their new home.

Coming to America: A Journey of Faith

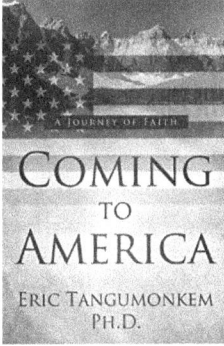

Do you struggle with trusting God with your finances? Feel that God is calling you to do something big but you can't see how it will be accomplished? Fear that He has abandoned you after starting your journey of faith? Coming to America: A Journey of Faith is Eric Tangumonkem's story of wrestling with these thoughts and doubts. God called him to America from Cameroon to pursue graduate studies at the University of Texas at Dallas, but he had no money to put towards this dream. In this book, Tangumonkem shares his journey of learning to trust God as he stepped out in faith and came to America despite a lack of funds. He also shares some of his formative experiences prior to this call-experiences that will encourage readers in their faith. Tangumonkem's life is a testimony to the faithfulness of God, and he is careful to give Him all of the glory.

The Use and Abuse of Titles in The Church

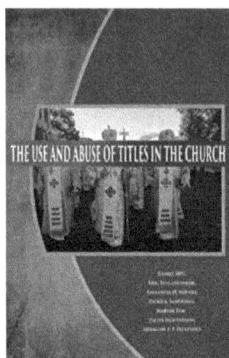

This book examines reasons behind the disturbing proliferation of titles in Christendom in recent times by seven distinguished Christian professionals. The book challenges readers to stay on the straight and narrow road, which celebrates ministers with titles bestowed based on sound Biblical foundations, while shunning those with titles associated with self-promotion and doctrinal errors. The book also provides the following actionable insights: · How to identify the proper use of titles · A history on the use of titles in Christendom How to avoid the pitfalls of acquiring bogus titles An understanding of the relationship between titles and leadership

Seven Success Keys Learned From My Father

This is a book about my father, my teacher, my role model and hero. A man of passion like any other man, but a man of exceptional qualities and abilities as well. The following are the seven keys to success my father passed to me: Fear of God, Humility, Education, Integrity, Hard work, Prayer and Vision. All these keys have been instrumental in making me who I am today. In addition to these keys, my father was present when we were growing up. He made it a point of duty to talk the talk and walk the walk before us. This book illustrates how these seven keys to success were interwoven in our day-to-day lives and how they have opened unprecedented doors of success to me. My sincere prayer for you as you read this book is that these keys will open all doors for you and bring the success you desire so strongly. Amen!

Viajando a America: Un Camino de Fe (Spanish Edition)

¿Lucha con confiar en Dios con sus finanzas? Siente que Dios le está llamando a hacer algo grande, pero usted no puede ver la forma en que se llevará a cabo? ¿Teme a que Él le ha abandonado después de comenzar su camino de fe?

Viajando a América: Un Camino de Fe es la historia de Eric Tangumonkem, de su lucha con estos pensamientos y dudas. Dios lo llamó a América desde Camerún para realizar estudios de posgrado en la Universidad de Texas en Dallas, pero no tenía dinero para seguir este llamado. En este libro, Tangumonkem comparte su viaje de aprender a confiar en Dios cuando caminó en la fe y llegó a Estados Unidos a pesar de su falta de fondos. También comparte algunas de sus experiencias formativas previas a esta convocatoria-experiencias que estimularán a los lectores en su fe. La vida de Tangumonkem es un testimonio de la fidelidad de Dios, y él tiene cuidado en darle toda la.

MON ODYSEE AMERICAINE: UNE EXPERIENCE DE FOI (French Edition)

As-tu du mal à confier tes soucis financiers au Seigneur? Ressens-tu que Dieu t'appelle à faire quelque chose de grand, mais tu ne sais comment cela va se réaliser? Crains-tu qu'il va t'abandonner en chemin? Mon Odyssée Américaine: une expérience de foi est l'histoire d'Éric Tangumonkem et de sa lutte contre le doute et les pensées susmentionnées. Dieu l'a appelé depuis le Cameroun pour aller poursuivre ses études supérieures à l'Université du Texas à Dallas, mais il n'avait pas d'argent pour réaliser ce rêve. Dans ce livre, le Dr Tangumonkem partage avec vous les péripéties de son voyage qui l'ont amené à faire davantage confiance à Dieu alors qu'il se rendit aux États-Unis par la foi. Il partage également certaines des expériences qui l'ont bâti avant même son appel –expériences qui vont encourager les lecteurs dans leur foi. La vie du Dr Tangumonkem est un témoignage de la fidélité de Dieu à qui il rend toute la gloire.

God's Supernatural Agenda: 7 Secrets to Lasting Wealth and Prosperity

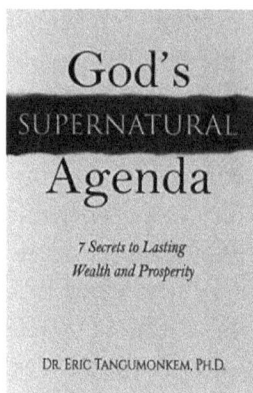

Is there something more valuable than money, precious stones, silver, and gold? Do you desire to be wealthy and prosperous? Are you already wealthy and prosperous, yet you feel empty and unsatisfied? Are you uncomfortable talking about money because it is "the root of all evil"? This book will not present shortcuts or get-rich-quick schemes, but important principles, laws, and processes involved in generating lasting wealth. You see, God desires for ALL of us to prosper today and for all eternity. He has a divine reason for that desire, and He has given us the way to attain it. God's Supernatural Agenda: 7 Secrets to Lasting Wealth and Prosperity presents His blueprint for prosperity and explains why it is what truly matters.

Racism, Where Is Your Sting? A provocative look at the beginning and the end of racism

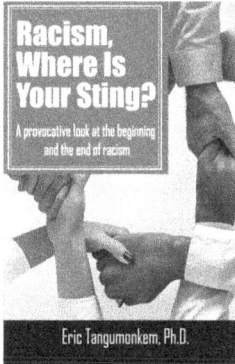

Each time the issue of racism is mentioned, tensions immediately run high, reason is thrown out the window, and emotional outbursts run rampant. Even though a lot of effort has been done to fight it, the devastating consequences continue to this day.

In this book, Dr. Tangumonkem challenges the status quo and presents a perspective that is both provocative and inspirational. Contrary to what you hear from those stoking the flames of racism and fermenting hate and bigotry, we are not at the mercy of racism. In fact, he dives deep into history to explain why the tendency to be racist is present in each one of us, regardless of skin color. The good news is that the victory has already been won — all we need is to live it out. When we stare right at this supercharged issue with fresh, unfiltered eyes, a seismic shift happens. Perhaps, the light at the end of racism is in sight.

IEM PRESS

To order additional copies of this book,
call 317-975-0806
or visit www.iempublishing.com

If you enjoyed this quality custom-published book,
drop by our website for more books and information.

"Inspiring, equipping, and motivating one author at a time."

www.ingramcontent.com/pod-product-compliance
Lightning Source LLC
Chambersburg PA
CBHW032117280326
41933CB00009B/875